W9-ATF-152

THE BLIND GUARDS OF EASTER ISLAND

By

Miriam Weiss Meyer

A
cpi
Book

From

RAINTREE CHILDRENS BOOKS
Milwaukee • Toronto • Melbourne • London

8 9 10 11 12   89 88 87 86 85

Library of Congress Number: 77-14529

Art and Photo Credits

Cover photo and photos on pages 15, 17, and 47, Annan Photo Features/Photo Trends.
Photos on pages 8, 23, 31, 32, 35, and 39, Wide World Photos, Inc.
Photo on page 10, Wide World Photos/Al Fusco.
Photo on page 13, Culver Pictures, Inc.
Photo on pages 18, 26, 37, and 44, Luis Villota/Bruce Coleman, Inc.
Photo on page 21, George Dineen/Photo Researchers, Inc.
Photo on page 27, George Holton/Photo Researchers, Inc.
Photos on pages 40 and 45, courtesy of the American Museum of Natural History.
All photo research for this book was provided by Sherry Olan.
Every effort has been made to trace the ownership of all copyright material in
this book and to obtain permission for its use.

Library of Congress Cataloging in Publication

Meyer, Miriam Weiss, 1927-
    The blind guards of Easter Island.
    SUMMARY: Discusses the human-like rock structures on Easter
Island and speculates on how they may have gotten there.
    1. Easter Island—Antiquities—Juvenile literature. 2. Man,
Prehistoric—Easter Island—Juvenile literature. 3. Easter
Island—History—Juvenile literature. [1. Easter Island—Antiquities.
2. Man, Prehistoric—Easter Island] I. Title.
F3169.M47   996'.18   77-14529

Manufactured in the United States of America
ISBN 0-8172-1048-2 lib. bdg.
ISBN 0-8172-2155-7 softcover

CONTENTS

Chapter 1

DISCOVERING THE EASTER ISLAND MYSTERY

The year is 1722. It is early spring—Easter time. The place is somewhere in the endless waters of the South Pacific. Three ships have sailed a thousand miles of ocean without sight of land. Their crew is searching for islands rich in foods, fruits, tobacco, minerals—anything that can be traded in the markets of Europe. The ships fly Dutch flags. Below their national flags are those of the *Dutch West India Company*—one of the largest merchant sailing fleets in the world.

The sailors are tired, badly sunburned, and bored. Suddenly, from his perch high atop the sails and rigging lines, the lookout on the lead ship calls out, *"Land ho! Land ho! To the north, sir. Land!"* The men on deck look up and begin to cheer. Admiral Jakob Roggeveen, stern commander of the three ships, calls for quiet. He turns his glass toward the north and sees the shadowy form of an island.

"Impossible," Admiral Roggeveen says, looking at his maps. "There is no island in this part of the ocean!" But the impossible has happened. He looks again through his glass. "Steer north," he shouts to the helmsman, "and signal the others to follow our sail. I have to see more of this island that shouldn't be where it is!" With that order a Dutch admiral moved the world toward a mystery that has gone unsolved for more than 250 years. Admiral Roggeveen would soon land on an unknown island whose people live with ancient secrets no human being has ever been able to unlock.

As the Dutch ships approached the cliff-bound coast, they fought a heavy surf that crashed against the rocky shore. But the dangerous surf wasn't what interested Roggeveen and his crew. It was the island itself that amazed them. This unknown island had huge stone walls all along the coast. On top of the walls were gigantic stones. Each stone was carefully carved in the shape of a human head. On many of the heads were enormous red stone caps.

When they were close to the sandy shore, the Admiral and his men saw that the walls were really stone platforms. And these platforms with their stone giants on top were everywhere on the island. There were hundreds of them! Admiral Roggeveen wrote in his ship's log: "They are remarkably tall stone figures that caused us to be filled with wonder."

Admiral Roggeveen ordered his men to stay on their ships until the next morning. Shortly after dawn, he went ashore to meet the islanders. According to his log, Admiral Roggeveen noticed several strange things about the people. Many of them wore large pieces of wood in holes cut through their earlobes. The wood stretched the earlobes so far that they dangled to their shoulders.

As he expected in this part of the world, the people were brown-skinned with black hair. But, strangely, there were others who were white-skinned, bearded, and had red hair. Admiral Roggeveen couldn't understand where

Tall and silent, the stone statues of
Easter Island have stood for centuries.

the white-skinned natives came from and why only they wore beards.

The Dutch Admiral was not interested in solving the mystery of this "island of the stone statues." The statues were of no value to the Dutch West India Company. The Company had sent him out to the Pacific to find trading posts. So he named the place Easter Island, in honor of the day on which he had discovered it. Roggeveen then sailed off—calmly turning his back on the stones that a half century later would touch off a mystery that has puzzled the world ever since.

Fortunately, later explorers who came upon Easter Island would ask more questions about the island's mysterious statues. Who were the ancient sculptors who carved the huge statues that weigh anywhere from 5 to 70 tons? (Some are as tall as a four-story house.) How were they built so high with only the hand tools that were used thousands of years ago? How had these giant statues been placed on their platforms? How did they place the red hats (each weighing between two and ten tons) on the giants' heads? Why were only *some* of the statues wearing them? And why did *all* the statues have those long earlobes?

Easter Island is a small South Pacific island now owned by Chile. It is a triangle-shaped island, 14 miles long and 7 miles wide. At each corner of the triangle is a dead volcano, each with a lake at its bottom. The island lies 2,300 miles west of the coast of South America. Easter Island hardly seems a likely place for ancient artists to have lived. The island sits alone like a tiny dot in the Pacific.

Easter Island sits alone—a tiny dot of land in the vast Pacific Ocean—2,300 miles west of Chile.

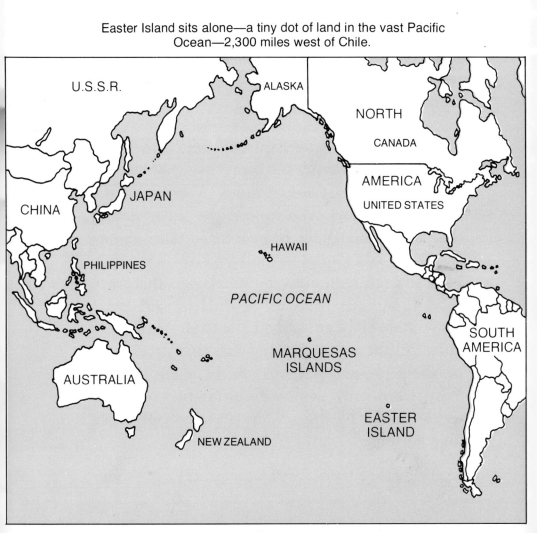

Easter Island—a pebble in 1,000 square miles of open ocean—could never have had a population of more than 4,000 people. Getting enough to eat could not have been easy for even so few people on this barren land. Its climate is not warm and sunny like most of the South Seas. The smashing surf must have made fishing dangerous. Yet the ancient natives of this island in the middle of nowhere found the time, the energy, and the desire to carve hundreds of stone giants. And then they found the means to set the giants on high stone altars around the coast of the island. *How ? Why? Who?*

And why do the giant heads not look like the brown-skinned people normally found in this part of the Pacific?

Chapter 2

THE MYSTERY GROWS

The man who discovered Hawaii, the famous Captain James Cook, arrived at Easter Island in 1774. He reported something strange aside from the building of the ancient statues. In Captain Cook's log we find a new mystery. Why had so many of the giant statues fallen from their altars? They all lay face down in the earth. Several of them had been broken. It was obvious to Captain Cook that the statues had been overturned, perhaps by the very people who built them.

Captain James Cook (1728-1779)—a British explorer—was the first to chart a useful map of the South Pacific. He predicted the discovery of Antarctica and discovered the Hawaiian Islands where he was killed while trying to find a boat that was stolen from him.

There were several artists with Captain Cook's sailing crew. The artists made drawings of the fallen statues. They also made sketches of some of the people living on the island. All the pictures showed the amazing, shoulder-length earlobes that Admiral Roggeveen had described a year earlier.

Captain Cook found it hard to imagine how the islanders could have lifted such enormous stone figures into place. They had no machines, no metal, and only the simplest tools. Cook could not even find trees that the islanders might have used to make wooden rollers to transport or lift the statues.

Captain Cook and his crew had many more questions about the great statues on Easter Island. Who had smashed statues that must have taken great time, work, and skill to carve? Who were the master builders? Why were the statues built in the first place? Cook could not find a single answer. If there were people on the island who knew the secrets of the stone statues, they certainly were not telling their secrets to strangers.

A small part of the Easter Island mystery was solved in the 1800s when the birthplace of all the giant statues was discovered. It was in the crater of one of the three dead volcanoes on the island—the crater of Rano Raraku.

Rano Raraku is one of the strangest places on earth. From the hard lava rock of this volcano came all of the stone for the Easter Island statues. Inside the volcano there still lie unfinished statues. Some are mere outlines. Others have been half-completed. Still others are completed but remain attached to the walls of the volcano by a small piece of rock at their backs.

These Easter Island statues on the slopes of the Rano Raraku volcano look small when seen from a distance . . .

All of the statues at Rano Raraku have the same deep-set, closed eyes. It seems the eyes were "opened" only when the statues were ready to be placed on their altars. All have the same long, pointed noses, the same thin, sneering lips, and the same long earlobes. There are more than 200 statues still in the volcano crater. All of them are enormous—the tallest measure almost 70 feet.

Could all of this remarkable work have been done by ancient people using only simple stone tools? Explorers found thousands of picks around Rano Raraku that were made from a very hard, black stone known as *obsidian*. Thousands of these picks were found near the site of the volcano. They looked as if they had been dropped by workers who quit or were called off the job. The same thing was found at a stone quarry seven miles away where the huge, red stone hats were made. There, too, all work seems to have suddenly stopped. Why weren't the stone statues completed? What made the ancient workers stop?

The statues that *were* completed, weighing up to 40 tons each, had to be carried down from the top of the crater. William J. Thomson, an

. . . . but, standing next to them, their huge size (23 feet tall and 23 feet under the ground) makes one wonder how they were ever built—and why.

American scientist who spent 12 days exploring Easter Island in 1886, could only write: "We were unable to arrive at any satisfactory conclusion as to how the immense statues on the upper tier of works could be moved to the plain below." *No one else has discovered the secret either.*

After a statue was carried down from the crater to the foot of the volcano, it was placed in a hole on the outer slopes. From there the statue would have to be moved to one of the stone altars. The trip might be as long as ten miles.

An unfinished statue lies, still attached to the stone walls of the volcano from which it was carved.

Over 70 of these completed statues stand in lines at the foot of the inner and outer slopes of Rano Raraku. Left there thousands of years ago, the statues have been buried up to their necks in shifting sands. All that can be seen of them are the famous heads that have come to identify Easter Island to the world. With their unseeing eyes, the statues will sit there for all time—*The Blind Guards of Easter Island.*

Pierre Loti, a writer who visited the island in 1872, wrote of the blind guards: "They frighten . . . They really don't have any bodies . . . . What do they represent, with their pointed noses and their thin lips that show a pout of disdain? . . ."

Loti also touches upon another part of the Easter Island mystery. He mentions some remarkable *paved roads* that seem to lead straight out of the sea. As Captain Cook had, Loti found the island littered with fallen statues along the shore. The statues had also been overturned along roads that were built from the shore, as though leading from the water! Every statue lay face down and pointing away from the sea. But *why?*

Chapter 3

CLUES FROM THE ISLAND'S LEGENDS

In 1935 Father Sebastian Englert arrived on Easter Island. He was to become one of the world's greatest experts on Easter Island. Father Sebastian was a monk who had been born and raised in Germany. He had planned to stay on the island for six months—just long enough to learn the native language and set up a school to teach the natives about Christianity.

Father Sebastian's "visit" lasted 35 years. In that time he collected the legends of the people and wrote them all down. The Easter Islanders

Father Sebastian Englert, with one of the very few
wood statues of Easter Island.

grew to trust and love him. They told him things about their history never told to another foreigner. They told him Easter Island legends never before written, but which were passed from parents to children over the centuries since the statues were built.

Among the legends was that of Hotu Matua. Hotu Matua was a great king who left his island homeland of Hiva. He left Hiva after he had been defeated in a war. Hotu Matua sailed toward the sun, taking with him 300 of his people. It is probable that Hotu Matua landed on Easter Island somewhere between 800 and 1200 A.D.

He is said to have brought to the new homeland many plants. Among these were the sweet potato, the bottle gourd (a large kind of pumpkin which was used to hold water), and the totora reed. The totora reed still grows in the lakes at the bottom of each of the three dead volcanoes on Easter Island. This reed was used to make canoes and the sides of houses.

When Hotu Matua was dying, he divided Easter Island among his four sons. Each son would rule his own part of the island. After a time, there were eight separate kin or family

Unlike Easter Island, Nuka Hiva and the other Hiva Islands to the northwest are covered with plant life and trees. Nuka Hiva is part of the Marquesas Islands, a French island group.

groups. Each group had its own leaders. Each leader had his share of farmers, craftsmen, and priests.

Some time after the arrival of Hotu Matua and his people, another group arrived at Easter Island. These were heavy-set men with long ear-lobes. They brought no women with them.

These natives became known as the *Long Ears*. These Long Ears took wives from the Hotu Matuas. Their wives and their children also became Long Ears.

The length of earlobes on the statues is probably an important clue in the mystery of who carved them. Since all of the giant stone statues have long earlobes, the sculptors were probably the Long Ears. The Short Ears may have been slaves forced by the Long Ears to work on the statues. By working together, the islanders managed to build statues and altars and to somehow feed all of the people. With a population of not more than 4,000, it took several generations to build one statue. An islander might have worked a lifetime on a statue without ever seeing the finished head.

But the building period on Easter Island that started around 1100 A.D. came to a sudden end. Again, legend offers an explanation of what happened. It tells of a revolt by the Short Ears against their long-eared rulers. Legend says that the Long Ears wanted the stones all over the island to be picked up and thrown into the sea. That way there would be more room to plant food.

Of course, the Long Ears expected the Short Ears to do the picking up and throwing. And, of course, the Short Ears refused. They said: "We discovered this island. Our great King Hotu Matua was a Short Ear."

The Long Ears had reason to think that the Short Ears were planning to kill them. So the Long Ears moved to a part of the island known as the Poike Peninsula. With the sea surrounding them on three sides, the Long Ears only had to worry about defending the side that was connected to the land. Across this two-mile strip they dug a deep trench and filled it with dry brush. If the Short Ears attacked, they would set fire to the brush and burn up the Short Ears.

But the Short Ears tricked the Long Ears. They somehow threw the Long Ears into the flaming ditch. The legend says: "They threw the Long Ears into the ditch, as if they were stones. They threw them down into the fires. The Long Ears were finished."

Strangely enough, the legend goes on to say the Short Ears took up the practice of lengthening *their* earlobes. This may account for the fact that the people who were seen by the early explorers like Admiral Roggeveen and Captain Cook had earlobes that were like slender cords hanging to their shoulders.

After the burning at Poike Ditch came a 200-year period known to the natives as the "Statue-Overthrowing Time." It lasted from about 1680 (the date of the fire) until about 1868.

Many of the Easter Island statues were broken or overturned in the Island war.

When the statues were overturned, it was the beginning of terrible times for the Easter Islanders. Family fought family and one person's flesh was eaten by another for revenge. One island cave from that period is known as "The Cave Where People Are Eaten."

Why were the stone statues on the altars pulled down? Why were many of the altars destroyed? Perhaps it was plain revenge. The Short Ears wanted to destroy anything that reminded them of the hated Long Ears. Possibly destroying the statues would also destroy any supernatural power they might have had.

Chapter 4

MODERN VISITORS AND THEIR THEORIES

In 1955 a man arrived on Easter Island with just one goal—*to solve the mystery of the blind guards.* He was the well-known Norwegian explorer and archaeologist—Thor Heyerdahl.

Heyerdahl believed that the earliest people to settle the islands of Polynesia (including Easter Island) were from South America. He believed those people were the Incas, people who ruled ancient Peru, Ecuador, and Chile. Heyerdahl set out to prove that it would have been possible for the ancient Incas to sail across the Pacific from the coast of Peru to Polynesia.

Heyerdahl had studied the history of Easter Island. He tried to fit the clues together. Before the Incas, the people of ancient Peru had white skin, beards, red hair, and long earlobes. The Incas had remembered these as the people who had taught them how to build huge stone structures. But the white-skinned, red-haired people left Peru when the Incas came to power. According to Incan legend, they sailed off into the ocean in the direction of the setting sun. That would be *west*–the direction of Easter Island. But could they have sailed such a long way in their simple boats?

Along with other scientists, Heyerdahl built a raft similar to those he had seen in drawings left by ancient Incas. The raft that was built was called *Kon-Tiki*.

Heyerdahl set out in the *Kon-Tiki* to prove that it was possible for the Incas to have sailed their rafts across thousands of miles of open sea.

He did just that, arriving on the South Sea island of Puka Puka, 101 days after starting the trip.

Thor Heyerdahl, a Norwegian explorer, sailed to Easter Island on the *Kon Tiki*—a raft he built to prove that people from ancient South America could have sailed to the island in just the same kind of boat.

Heyerdahl's trip from Peru to Easter Island took 101 days
through the shark-filled Pacific Ocean.

To find out how the statues were moved from their birthplace in Rano Raraku, Heyerdahl enlisted the help of Mayor Atan of Easter Island. The Mayor was supposed to be a descendant of the original Long Ears.

According to Mayor Atan, each statue was placed on a heavy, Y-shaped tree branch that formed a kind of sled. Then the statue was tied to the branch with strong ropes. Another rope was placed around the statue's neck. Many people, sometimes 100 or more, then pulled on the rope. If this story is true, there must have been trees on Easter Island at one time.

The Mayor gathered 180 men and women. He tried to have them move a ten-ton statue in the way he had described. And it worked! As the 180 people pulled on the rope, the huge statue began to move. The sled on which it rested bumped across the rocky road.

Heyerdahl also was able to prove how a statue, once it had been dragged to its altar, was then placed on top of the altar. Again, it was the Mayor who showed how it was done. At a place called Anakena a statue weighing 25 tons had been pulled from its altar.

Could Mayor Atan lift it and put it back onto its altar? Heyerdahl says he did. He got 12 people to help. They brought three wooden poles and a pile of stones. The method was simple and clever. The three poles were pushed under the statue's face. Then the Mayor's helpers leaned on the poles. The poles acted as levers and raised the statue's face up. Then the Mayor pushed small stones under the head. This was repeated until, after a while, the head sat on a pile of stones about three feet high.

After 18 days of this back-breaking work— lifting the carved rock inch by inch—the statue was ready to be placed once again on its altar.

Once the statue had been lifted into place this way, it became possible to see how the red hats called *topknots* had been placed on the heads. Using the same pile of stones that had been placed under the statue, the topknots were rolled up the ramp and onto the heads. Ropes tied around them helped to get them up the ramp of stones.

Next, Heyerdahl and his archaeologists turned their attention to finding dates for some

After 18 days of lifting, Mayor Atan's crew raised the statue as high as its platform. The statue at Anakena stands today as a landmark that can be seen far out to sea.

of the legends. Using a chemical dating method, Heyerdahl proved that the altars had been built long before the statues, and by a *different* peo-

ple. The altar building probably began some-
time around 850 A.D., while the earliest date of
the statue carving is around 1200 A.D.

Heyerdahl and his archaeologists then went
to the Poike Peninsula where a great burned-out
trench was located. Could this be the site of the
great Poike Ditch Fire of the "Long Ear-Short
Ear" legend? Father Sebastian had calculated
from legends that the fire in which the Long
Ears burned had taken place in 1680.
Heyerdahl's scientists proved that a great fire
had burned in the Poike Ditch in 1676! Perhaps
the legend was not a legend. Perhaps Father
Sebastian had been given important historical
facts.

Dr. William Molloy, a scientist working
with Thor Heyerdahl, came across another important clue while digging at the altars one day.
He found some stonework that reminded him of
the stonework he had seen high in the Andes
Mountains in Peru. He believed these stone-
works had been built by those pre-Incas with the
red hair who had sailed into the sunset.

Heyerdahl became quite excited. He now
was becoming more and more certain that the

The Heyerdahl group came across Easter Island stone buildings
that are much like those they had seen in the
Andes Mountains of Peru.

earliest settlers of Easter Island had come from
Peru. In addition to the stone altars, he offered
as evidence the following:

- The sweet potatoes that are eaten by all
  the people of Easter Island are found no-

where else in Polynesia. They are eaten in South America.

- The totora reed that grows at the bottom of the crater lakes of all three of the dead volcanoes of Easter Island is found at Lake Titicaca high in the Andes of Bolivia on the border of Peru.

- The early settlers of Easter Island had long ears. The pre-Incas of Peru also practiced the lengthening of their earlobes.

- Some of the early settlers of Easter Island had fair skin and red hair. The same is true of the pre-Incas.

Dr. Edwin Ferdon, another archaeologist on the Heyerdahl Expedition, found a wall painting in a cave on Easter Island that showed a crescent-shaped boat with square sails. It was exactly like the boats used by the people of Lake Titicaca in Peru.

These boats, the legends said, had been used by those same red-haired, fair-skinned people who had left after the Incas arrived. The boats had been made of woven totora reeds.

In the Lake Titicaca area of Peru, totora reed boats are made by all the local families. The boats, made just as they were thousands of years ago, last only a few years before sinking to the bottom of the lake.

These boats were certainly sturdy enough to carry huge stones across Lake Titicaca. Why couldn't they have been used by the early Easter

Islanders to transport the heavy, red-stone topknots from the quarry to the altars? The remains
of the roads going down to the sea could have

How could people on a treeless island carve this *wood* statue of
a human-like bird? Could there have been trees on Easter Island
at one time?

been roads that led to landing places on the shore.

A legend states that once the island had many tree-shaded roads. There is evidence that long ago there were, indeed, trees on the island. And Thor Heyerdahl conducted pollen tests that proved trees once grew on Easter Island.

Chapter 5

MORE PROOF, MORE THEORIES

One of the most important finds made by the Heyerdahl group was a strange statue.They found it at the foot of one of the slopes at the cliffs of Rano Raraku. It was like no other statue that had ever been found on Easter Island.

The statue was of a kneeling man, with short ears, a beard, and a round head. It was a complete figure, not just a statue from the hips up. The kneeling man was resting on his heels. The figure weighed only about ten tons. That was small compared with the 50-ton statues found on the island.

Heyerdahl and others recognized the figure. They had seen such statues high up in the Andes near Lake Titicaca. Could this statue be further proof of Heyerdahl's theory that the earliest Easter Islanders had come from South America?

Heyerdahl's expedition had uncovered some remarkable information. But none of it could be proved. And many questions still remained unanswered. The Norwegian's theories were not accepted by most archaeologists.

First of all, if the altars had been built by a separate group of people, which group had built the statues? Were they the followers of Hotu Matua? Hotu Matua was supposedly a Short Ear. Why would Short Ears build statues of Long Ears? Besides, the language spoken by the Easter Islanders is a Polynesian language. There is no trace of a South American Indian language in the Easter Island dialect.

Other scientists say Hiva, according to legend the place from which Hotu and his followers came, is probably an actual island to the *west* of Easter Island. There are three such islands.

The statue of a kneeling man with short ears, round head, and a beard was found. It is the only one of its kind ever found on Easter Island.

There is another theory for the carving of the Easter Island statues. In a book written in 1970, *Chariots of the Gods,* author Erich von Daniken asks whether or not the Easter Island heads might have been carved to resemble ancient visitors from other planets. He sees a relationship between the Nazca lines in Peru and the Easter Island statues. This is also discussed in *The Case of the Ancient Astronauts,* a 1977 book by I.J. Gallagher.

The visitors from outer space may have been thought to be gods by the humans who greeted

The "bird people" of Easter Island are rock carvings that might be a clue to ancient visitors thought to come from the skies.

them. Is it possible there were such visits to our planet by other-world creatures in ancient times? Could they have taught some ancient earthlings the mathematics, science, and building methods that humans could not themselves have known at that time? It is a far-fetched theory, but perhaps no stranger than the many mysteries surrounding Easter Island.

Four years after Heyerdahl left Easter Island, two of the scientists who were with him on his visit returned to the island. Like many others who have explored Easter Island they just couldn't stay away.

It took the returning scientists eight months to repair an altar that had been badly damaged. During these months they lifted seven huge statues into place. They used no modern machines, but relied on the ancient method that had been shown to them years before by Mayor Atan.

Other scientists and explorers have returned to Easter Island. Most have gone back for answers to their endless questions, but many have also helped to lift the statues back into place. Year by year the toppled statues are re-

Seven of the "Blind Guards of Easter Island," once again watch over their ancient birthplace.

turned to their altars and Easter Island's blind guards stand watch once again. And year by year more questions are asked about what these ancient statues would tell us if they only could.

None of the questions, then, about who came to Easter Island and when, have really been answered. We don't know why the statues were built or who built them. We don't know why they were overturned. Tourists and scientists continue to visit the island to stand open-mouthed before the great statues that still face the vast Pacific. To some, these Blind Guards of Easter Island will always be frightening. To others, they will almost certainly remain one of the world's great unsolved mysteries.